by Douglas King

Poems in a Minor Chord
The Curmudgeon's Guide to Gratitude
You May be Old If

vicious circles

First published in the United States of America in 2022 by

Day III Productions, Inc.
www.DayIIIProd.com

Copyright © 2022 by Douglas King. All rights reserved. Printed in the United States of America. No part of this book, whole or in part, may be used or reproduced in any manner whatsoever, without the written permission except in the case of reprints in the context of reviews.

Cover Enso by Taido Shufu (1776 - 1836)

ISBN: 978-1-7376256-3-6

vicious circles

by
douglas king

introduction

We ridicule and chastise certain bad behavior but then turn right around and celebrate it. We make heroes of outsiders and criminals to the point that they become the insiders and the rest of the world becomes the outsiders.

If you don't care who is in or out of society, and carry yourself with a punk nonchalant, "I'm too cool for this" attitude, that would make you out and being outside then makes you inside. For it's the outside who make it inside. We love these Cinderella stories and Hollywood produces movies and documentaries about such characters, which only reinforces the notion that they are in.

What does this cult of celebrity illustrate to children who hear of or watch the Netflix documentaries and docudramas? What lessons about society and culture do they learn and then act upon as they grow older trying to find their place in the world? Are we simply creating a culture of Insta-celebrities that we love to build up only to tear down?

Sounds like a vicious circle. Hence the title of this collection of poems, predominately written during the time of isolation between 2020 and 2021 when the world was in the midst of a global pandemic.

Discussed in this collection are topics such as the process of writing, the solitary and often emotional life of an artist, mental health, love, and sexuality. In some cases, the poems take on a retro 70s vibe ala Jim Morrison or John Lennon (two influences) as the subconscious mind takes lead. Where it leads is anyone's guess.

I think it is safe to say that all of us want to feel important, be taken seriously for our opinion and work, and ultimately, we all want to leave a mark that we existed and meant something to this world after we are gone. The collection before you explore these themes and is my attempt of leaving my mark.

There are moments of great fertility
the mind a bountiful garden
blooming thoughts
ripe with meaning
words as nectar
sweet to ears
life-affirming
a soil teeming with nutrients
of song
        verse
                theme
                        prose
drink deeply of me
harvest the richness
seeded in seasons past
to produce such a lush yield
for all to partake
to feast
        indulge
                satisfy
                        satiate

Timber
she cried out
on my behalf

that's a good friend
who's there with you
in the end

so they say
as I splinter
from desire

crashing
mentally, physically
emotionally, spiritually

a squirrel runs pass
catching your attention

What do you want
caviar and escargot,
notoriety and acknowledgment,
fortune and fame,
awards and accolades,
to be left alone,
to be free to just be you?
what do you yearn for,
glory and attention,
invites and opportunities,
respect and consideration,
parties and women,
to be at peace
with all and yourself?

the milk in the fridge
it has soured

I can only be me
it's all I know how to be
it's all I've ever been
what do I do
when it's not enough?
how do I become
someone other than me?
would I want to?

the duck passes the swan on glassy lake
concerned only to find food

Force
not inspiration
still creation

exaltation
a motivation
for promotion
need prioritization

black scratches
scars of emotion
escaping from nib

darkness
swirling head
hope and dread

themes
no end in sight
countless circles

stop it
just
stop it

the bread layered green with mold
from neglect

QUESTIONS NO. 1

Am I anti-social
because I was shunned
or was I shunned
because I was anti-social?

who's to blame?
is there blame?

I prefer being alone
but is that only
because I am alone?

when can I get off this ride?
I'm not enjoying it
but is enjoyment
the purpose?

I want to live life
but I also like the life
I live

are happiness and contentment
just not meant for me?
or maybe I don't know how?

a squirrel always
searches for a nut

QUESTIONS NO. 2

What will it take to make you happy?
I do not know

why can't you let it go?
I do but it's holding on to me

do you enjoy being this way?
does a salmon enjoy being eaten by the bear?

do you want to be set free?
yes, please, show me the key

the jailer is imprisoned
as much as the criminal

I write words
that's what I do
I wrote these words
and give them to you

these words I give
with much love
these words I hope
you will want more of

these words
are yours now
you can love them
or hate them if you shall

I will always
write more
my mind always at play
writing never a chore

I'll leave you
with my final rhyme
reading these words
was hopefully an enjoyable time

This world's not for me
nor I for it
I produce the same as others
but mine is considered shit

get over yourself
you sniveling whiner
you compare yourself to artists
when merely an outlier

my case is made
for all to see
it won't make a difference
I am not received

stop your crying
not everyone has success
not when a few
decide what is best

the system is broken
and too blind to care
it feeds itself
not meant to be fair

You get real with someone
but that comes back on you
they betray your trust
or judge you
and you just take it
that's life
that's why it is so difficult to be real
so we hurt
and we hide
but it has to come out
so we trust
we get real with someone, again
and eventually, again, we will be betrayed
it's as inevitable
as the sun rising
death and taxes
yet we need to be true to ourselves
we are created to share

As with these words here

If left to my own devices
I will devise a way to be unhappy

it if comes down to me
I will come up with an excuse

if the decision lies with me
I will decide to be alone

what is wrong with me?
why am I this way?
maybe I was born this way.

the moon illuminates
the fog that enshrouds
my thinking

Who do I write these words for?
why do I ask these questions?
what is the point?

nihilism
fatalism
agnosticism

rolling thunder under my skull
piercing synapse
ruptured cortex

a mist enveloping
caressing with acid touch
penetrating with lies on quicksand

unplug me
reboot me
recycle me

triplets meant to set me free
stream of consciousness
for the unconscious

Clang clang
goes the thought
the inner cerebellum rot

whiz bang
pops the mind
a brain in noticeable decline

crackling thunder
spreads like spilled blood
across two hemispheres
the forced rhymes
signs of mental deterioration

Got to get you
out of my head
got to get peace, man
to fill it instead

but the you
is really me
got to get out
got to get free

release the madness
release the pain
write these words
may be judged insane

it's okay, it's all right
a couplet brings it all to an end tonight

When what you want
does not exist
you're left with
what you have

have and have not
simultaneous
Schrodinger's cat
two existences, one life

an imagination
so strong
it creates something impossible
making it possible

a desire
so powerful
it manifests a dream
unobtainable

what cruelty
this imagination

My pain
leaks as this ink
onto the page

taking shape
as tercets
forming a poem

the dreams
and desires
and goals

an unholy trinity
unachievable
more a nightmare

overly dramatic
this morose
but what I feel all the same

is a feeling truth?
what constitutes a reality?
should I just shut up and go to bed?

TRYING TO HAVE FUN

Porridge skies
clouds filled with eyes
a cheap rhyme
to pass the time
not at all sublime
an ongoing stanza
ostrich egg bonanza
how do I sleep at night?
in a bed just fine
don't rhyme every line
self-referential
the major differential
too clever and self-aware
too old and horny to care
not meant to be funny
the beat the force
a matter of meter, of course
a gummy bear riding a horse
across sparkling skies
clouds filled with eyes
a circular end
a bow that ties

Hear me
I write out to you
my stains searching
for receptive eyes
acknowledge me
a pathetic need
so deeply ingrained
I shrink from these words
validate me
shower me with praise
an embarrassing admission
the creator's curse

and then it's edited out anyway
censored and discarded

TIME

It's what we wish we had more of
but sometimes we have too much of
it equals money
it heals all wounds
there's never enough of it
yet we waste it every day
it hasn't been kind to us
but it's the best and the worse of
it flies
it stands still
it can get away from you
even when we hold on to it
give me a minute
a second
we cherish it when we're together
it ends when we're apart
time is on our side
time and time again
we're running out of it
soon
time will be up
the end will have come

Held together
with tape
and rubber bands
it's all I can do
to not float
into the void
and vacuum
of eternity

seeking, sought, sunk
can't escape this funk
my words nothing but junk

a brief rhythmic interlude
to break the monotony
of my melancholy

hold it together
no time to fall apart
there're others to consider
self-care
could be selfish
if left to its own devices

will time heal these wounds?
only time will tell

Fish in window
rubber girdle
women in swarms
scantly clad
on a banker's wages

hedge fund hussies
boys compensating
overstating
leaving their wives waiting
dry masturbating
this is all just irritating

pointless
meaningless
directionless
aimless
no remiss

words for word's sake
a word's worth
literal pictures
pictures of literacy
keeping the timing right

moistened butterfly wings
a sprouted seed
frosted windowpane
a freshly used toothbrush
rinsed and shelved for the night

Pounding from the inside to get out
shhhhhh, shhhhhh
be quiet for the night

set us free, set us free
we want to breath
we must spread and grow
multiplying, spawning

don't be so restless
I'm doing the best I can

we demand more
we will not be satisfied

even this poem
does not quench the hunger

These words lay on white graves
decomposing their composition
some smell, a stench
others the fragrance
of memorial flowers

these words are a healing balm to my psyche
a glass surface lake
some decry, cliché
others the poignant cry
of the soul

these words are comfort in the dark of night
the pale moon scarred
a faint light
ink and structure
of timeless emotions

No agenda
no schedule
no purpose
no intent
just life

pure creation
self-motivation
free innovation
peace sensation
just life

a time with no time
a time infinite
a moment
a time after time
just life

free from demands
free from responsibility
free from worry
free from stress
just life

hurl me into the infinite universe
let me experience the glory
of nothingness

I don't know
how to cry
for help any clearer

but my words
never heard
ignored, making room for other's feelings

we turn
a blind eye
we don't want to know

cover it up
be strong
keep pushing through

I can't anymore
don't you hear?
don't you care?

and yet, I do
keep going
pain never-ending

that's life

Call it a delusion
isn't every great innovation
first considered delusional?

the monumental heads of Rapa Nui
that can't be done
it's done

the precision of Manchu Pichu
that can't be done
it's done

a video store clerk becomes an Oscar-nominated
    director
that can't be done
it's done

an animated mouse builds an empire
that can't be done
it's done

a delusion
is simply greatness
waiting to occur

How fast is the clock ticking?
how quickly does the calendar change?
did someone set the clock ahead?
where does time fly to?

stop the planet
I want to get off
I need to catch up
I need to reset

is the earth spinning faster?
is our orbit shortening?
the days are getting shorter
it was only yesterday

stop the planet
I want to get off
I need to catch my breath
I need just a second

why do we set this maddening pace for ourselves?
who fired the starting pistol?
we're in control, but not

Formula 1 thoughts
oval track mind
consume to admire
produce and aspire

need time to produce
need money for time
press on due to passion
passion drives purpose

deep need for validation
overflowing with inspiration
all ideas can be brilliant
if perceived that way

these words complete a lap
they're in the race
round we go again
a track has no end

I believe
in a God
that doesn't believe
in me

no amount
of prayer
can penetrate
my invisibility

you can
in fact
hide a light
without need of a bushel

but why
would you
if you want
to be believed in?

Words, my ammo
firing blanks
no recoil
no wound inflicted
except to self
through ambivalence
the world's Kevlar

I am disarmed
but my clip is full
I lay awake
four am
a shot
into a cold windless night
no report
ignored

Struggle
so hard
to complete

always
swimming against
the rip tide

only
to finish
then be ignored

words
a wisp
whispered in a storm

ignored
globally undesired
no trace

how do you desire
what you don't know exists?

CAUGHT UP

I try to get caught up
        in my work life
I try to get caught up
        in my personal life

never enough time
always something to do
always something more
that's life

it's ongoing, never-ending, infinite
the point of the journey
is not to arrive
it's to survive

you never empty the inbox
it's bottomless
just as time is endless
you won't ever catch up

See me
I'm here
scratching these pathetic marks
like a scribbling mad man
in his stone prison cell

dare I
send out these missives
on wings of white doves
searching for land
a perch in someone's mind

dare you
partake in
the bitter fruit
of my thoughts
to fester or possibly fertilize

it's only
my cry for attention
a desperate
call for action
will you respond?

To get ahead in life
you have to work 24/7
to make the most of life
you have to play 24/7

to live your best life
you need time and money
to live a peaceful life
you abstain from earthly desire

you can have everything in life
live your life for yourself
have a meaningful life
sacrificing your life for others

you only have one life
live it to the fullest
or make a life worth remembering

I can write my words
for me
I can paint my art
for me
but that's not enough
for me

ego bursts
a blackhole
absorbing all matter
unquenchable hunger

if only you had a desire
for me
if only I was enough
for me
if only someone cared
for me

The same words
different writers
one is praised
the other is ignored

the measuring stick
is not the same
bitter or honest
critics decide

who elected the critic?
who wrote the rules?
where is the critic?
the writer kicks against the goads

let all be judged equally
or, let no judgement be passed
it's all the same
not one of the words has changed
(only in the process)

let it be
let it all be

Sunlight enters the room
on two legs
clear blue sky
in almond eyes
radiant and warming
my entire body
thirsts for more
like a blossom that leans to the sun
I am drawn to the source
a milky way of sparkles
with a simple smile
I am lost
adrift in endless space
don't attempt to rescue me
I don't want to be saved
I ripple with universal energy

Why do I do anything?
is it for others
or self?

others will always disappoint
self-serving
the opposite of how
life should be lived

everyone's looking out
for number one
so am I
I guess

To have a thing
you have to do something
anything
but well

even if it's not technically good
do it to the fullest
do it with all your heart

that will become your thing
spend time with your thing
study your thing
your thing should/will be a part of you

so, what's your thing?
this is mine

Version 1

To me you are perfect
One look is all I need

All you say delights me
No one compares
No, not one
Amusement you write

With your song I am lifted
In your smile is joy
Tell me you care
Hold my heart

Leave it whole
Oh, if only you knew
Verily, I say you are the one
Every day I pray the dream come true

Version 2

Tally the ways
Only you can please

All I seek
Never a doubt
Never a question
Always the answer

Where you are is joy
In you is peace
Through you is relief
Hope, I have

Love, you offer
Our time may come
Value you, I will
Every dream bears your name

It cost a lot
to look like shit
how does that make sense?

designer dirt
acid wash, distressed
holes don't come with wear but laser

if you are homeless
is it ironic
or couture?

when did street
become chic?
this ain't no diss

graffiti hangs in galleries
low = high
how do you tell the act from the fact?

do we even try?
why ask why?

I'm tired of feeling bad
I'm tired of feeling tired
I'm tired of feeling I'm not good enough
I'm tired of feeling like a failure
I'm tired of being compared
I'm tired of being worried
I'm tired of being afraid
I'm tired of being ignored

I'm tired of being told I'm not real enough
that my work has nothing to say
then why do I say it?

are there different rules for the world and for me?
how many can relate?
I'm not unique in feeling this way

aren't we all tired of doing this to each other?

String of words
where does your power come from?
is it imbued by the writer
or formed from your own existence
in the hands of Dickinson
you are art
the musing of Morrison
you are mastery
but an unknown
you are gibberish
is your power given to you?
your very soul empty and void of meaning
a canister in need of filling
then Yeats comes along
and gives you purpose
Frost, Angelou, Cummings, Ginsberg
without them, you are without meaning
devoid of purpose and power
all of this is nothing

I treat you bad
because I feel bad
which makes you feel bad
so then you treat me bad

I have to understand you
so you can understand me
I have to empathize with you
so you can empathize with me

we must have compassion for each other
so we can have compassion for each other
I have compassion for you
so you can have compassion for me

we must forgive each other
so we can forgive each other
I have to forgive you
so you can forgive me
then I will truly forgive you

we love each other
but we hurt each other
because of how much we love each other

why is it so difficult to be honest with each other?
to be honest with ourselves?
why is it so hard for us to accept and believe one another?

when humans stop being humane
do we lose our humanity?

What makes you happy
doesn't make me happy
but you want you to be happy

what's best for you
isn't what's best for me
but I want what's best for you

we love each other
but it's our love that keeps us apart

how can two be so right
and so wrong?
how do two positives
create a negative?

we each want the other to be happy
but to do so only leads
to both of us being sad

I'm buried
in a snow-covered grave
I'm resting
by a winter bald tree

echoes of long-lost dreams
dart to the heart

I'm feasting
at a royal banquet
I'm drunk
on revelry and mirth

illusions eclipsed my reality
shards of present possible outcomes

I'm happy
in my solitary confinement
I'm mad
in my padded cell

cascading delusions shatter
time of reflection coming to an end

Where are you?
I've been waiting
long, the wait

ruts of despair
gulley I've carved
treading my footsteps

come to me
illuminate
the path to you

I'm seeking you
a thread
thin among coarse wire

you I sought
desert found
footsteps in sand erased

I feel sorry for myself
someone has to
but I'm not someone
well, that's just more feeling sorry for myself

circular logic
lack of logic
distorted perspective

just go see a counselor already
give us all a break
and there I go again

Blogs are the twenty-first century equivalent
of a message in a bottle
self-publishing our memoirs
for narcissistic pleasure
because we think we matter
we have something to say
my words
my life
will change your life

the worst part
it's probably true

You want the through-line for my work?
how do all the styles connect?
you can't write poetry
and write scripts
and paint
and design
pick a discipline
you can't be so undisciplined
a jack of all trades
pick a lane
chose a motif
make up your mind
who do you want to be?
who are you?

you want a through-line for my work?
it's me

Hurting
I am hurting
there I said it
no symbolism
no metaphor
not trying to hide it
revealing my truth
I'm in pain
my emotions run like tap water
okay, one metaphor
none the less
I've spoken my truth
laid my heart open

now, what are you going to do?

Liquid shit
fire sprite
take a drink
on death's night

harvest moon
tepid tea
guzzling blood
the sane flee

tempest seas
open sore
sipping daiquiris
ignoble gore

raging hemorrhoid
fetid mind
pour another one
you're my kind

rotten eggs
for eyes to see
swallow the pill
there nothing here for me

By the world's standards
I am a failure
though I often aspire
to those standards
but by my standards
I have succeeded

deluded
or
saner than most?

the world says
to be a success
work 24/7
but the successful say
live and enjoy life
make the most of each day
which do I choose?

I want to do it all
experience it all
see it all
hear it all
visit everywhere
all at once
an exponential sensory supernova
big bang
alpha omega

a new beginning
then begin again

QUESTIONS NO. 3

Once something is made fun of and satirized
how does it keep going?

don't they know the world
is laughing at them?

don't they know we're all
in on their secret?

is it meant to be ironic?
or are they just moronic?

is the truth so difficult
to see?

QUESTIONS NO. 4

How will you be noticed?
make one thing as best as it can be
make a thousand things

quality vs. quantity
the quantity makes it quality
does it?
is a hundred pounds of shit still shit?

what if it's quality shit?
then the shit is no shit.
who gives a shit?

we all want to be more than shit
but the world makes us feel like shit
ain't that the shit?

Tell me no lies
when I am between your thighs
I only want to hear your sighs
don't tell me about the other guys
I can see them in your eyes
I thought we had no stronger ties

tell me no lies
tell me no lies

it's only my spirit that dies

You need to spend money
to make money
you need to produce product
to be able to produce product
you have to force to be seen
to be seen
you have to pay for likes
to be liked
advertise
promote
pay for reviews
pay for likes
pay to exhibit
pay to be in the game
when the game is to be paid
if you want
to be on top
you have to force
yourself up
from the bottom

Overnight sensation
the downfall
resurrection
rehab
the comeback
the relapse
destruction
rebuilt
the exposure
redemption

you're fallible
you're human
you're canceled
you're blacklisted
you're forgiven
you're martyred

we build-up
only so we can tear down

why do we do this to ourselves?
why do we do this at all?

I want to do something meaningful
of importance

is it for ego
or art sake?

a lasting imprint
that I existed
that I mattered
that I had meaning

When did everything become a crisis?
it rains and we have a weather alert!
people arrive at our borders
and it's an invasion!
a pandemic
a health warning
a systemic problem
an economic collapse
a war on drugs
a culture clash

the media is partially to blame
if it bleeds
it leads
no responsibility
in the name of the news

fake news
opinions
deep fakes
false information
conspiracies
gaslighting

no one is right
when everyone is wrong
now, that's a crisis!

Feet to the flame
feel the pain
the world insane

don't say this
don't say that
progressive
but regressive

vicious circles
catfish
gaslight
pick your poison
it all is

no one gets out alive
if we're all canceled
do we go into repeats and syndication?

when does it end
vicious circles

I want to do nothing
but my nothing always becomes something

to sit
is to read
is to write
is to watch
which becomes a task
                a chore
                a responsibility
it's no longer nothing
it has been imbued with meaning

to relax
is to become busy
mind racing
always calculating
always measuring
always planning
relaxing is tiring to the point of stress
it is pointless to hope for a different result
it is pointless trying to change

My depression stems from ego
ego to be recognized for
       my art
       my contribution
poetry is psychiatry
creativity is catharsis
meta
or narcissism
or both
clever
of trite
either way therapeutic
self-evaluation
introspection
which arose from the
realization that
my depression steams from ego

Words elude me right now
yet I write anyway
despite of
in spite of

11:22
pm
digital clock

it doesn't matter
no one will read this
anyway
anyways?

quatrain
tercet
quatrain

Billy asks for a twist ending
maybe meta will do
not bad
for having no words

Plunge into darkness
during wakefulness
revive during sleep

glass pipe
only reprieve
mow the lawn
prune the tree

bubbles bursting
mind thirsting
dance lady
dance

let your song sing
spread for joy
tall order
from short-order cook

rise up
kiss this guy
don't reason why
do it, he soon will die

Eyes blinded
with youth
beauty in the eyes of the beholder
not the beheld

youth has age cataracts
what is age?
discrimination is a two-way road
ageism is beheld in the mind of the afflicted

see me
I'm standing here
age is invisible
and so am I

Do you see me?
I see you
I see you

social constructs
social norms
social structures

age barriers
emotional barriers
social barriers

both ends of the spectrum
taboo
says who?

see the life in front of you
but it's not for you
and only a dream for me

Oh, Honey
a vagina is just a vagina
it's the heart and soul that matter

you can't tempt me
show me knowledge
show me compassion
don't show me flesh

oh, honey
you're so much more than your sex
I shouldn't even call you, Honey

Come out
come out
come out of your room
come out of your comfortable cocoon

it's time
it's time
it's time, don't be afraid
it's time that your future be made

come see
come see
come see what awaits you
come see all the marvelous things to do

you were born for such a time as this
you only need to step out
and step into your destiny
we long to see you in ecstasy

Rare is the person
who believes they are normal

we all desire to be special
unique
but this desire makes us not
special or unique
it's a loop
mobius strip
infinite cycle

I want to be special
to be thought highly of
for these very words
do they qualify?
did I make it?

so cliché
a poet not of note
so desperate to be noticed
aren't we all?
so, again, not unique
all the same

this is life
the cycle of life is made up of cycles
Venn diagrams that constitute our
existence

rare if the person
who just wishes they left no trace

Driven
passionate
to create
make a mark
leave a mark
a word
an image
a lasting impression
is it good?
was it worth it?
if a mark is made
and no one notices
was it a mark?

disappear

Impaired
in pairs

stanzas
tango

universal dance floor
beautiful whore

I want more
I've lost the score

they're just words
they come in herds

forcing it
flowing in it

please love me

Vaseline soaked gauze
peeking through
you attempt to see me

echoes of times since gone
reflections blurred
vapor trails you attempt to grab

a peripheral vision
I am to you
lost in near- and far-sightedness

we sit facing one another
but miles apart
lost in time forgotten

ODE TO SHIT

There is something earthy
about the smell

at first repugnant
at twice natural

not soothing
but essential

to life
to health

fertilizer
compost

Hello, friend
do you know me?
do you recognize these deep furrows on my brow?

they've been etched there
wondering if you would ever arrive

trenches of doubt
cartography of worry on the landscape of my face

is love unrequited
if only one person is involved?

a tree
growing alone
can still bud

I long to sleep
the endless sleep
forever lost in dreams

to wake
and surrender to life
is the nightmare

the deep well
of unconsciousness
beckons me forth

sink your fangs
deep into my wakefulness
drink deeply

rest my head
on pillows of hope
that this night I remain asleep

Pleasantly confused
the man is
sitting on a stump
waiting for order to return from chaos

thoughts creep
unfocused and untethered
lost like an echo
drifting, settling, alight again, forevermore

blank looks
eyes in distant stare
the man is unaware
hoping the light will return

Lennon got it
Harrison got it
Gaye got it
71
2021
we're still dealing with it
same shit
same shit
50 years
how do we not see?
how do we not hear?
imagine
isn't it a pity
what's going on
how can we still be so blind?
how can we be so deaf?
how can we be so hard?
it's true
those that don't learn
are bound to repeat

we're the proof

We have eyes to see
        but we are blind
we have ears to hear
        but we are deaf
we have sense to know right from wrong
        but we have no common sense

so flawed
imperfect, selfish, arrogant, vain, merciless

we have our own agenda
we don't care who it affects
we have our own beliefs
        we don't care whose freedom it robs
we have our own reason
        no matter how unreasonable

hopeless?
vocal, selfless, empathetic, humble, compassionate

No one knows
for sure
all the philosophers
professors
scientist
priests
all the concepts
thesis
theories
beliefs

they're all just guesses
nothing concrete
nothing perfected
no ultimate resolution

no one knows
for sure
so why get so worked up,
so bent out of shape,
so offended?
it's all just conjecture
go with it
just be

Clean up
erase any evidence I was here
no regret
transactional

spread like angel wings
you were
no desire
just action
some reaction

time is up
thanks for cumming
no, it wasn't a chore
I'll be forgotten
once I walk out the door

Happiness is not being
        happy
happiness is not needing
        to be happy
happiness is people
but people make me unhappy
because there are no people
alone

all happy thoughts are when
friends and family are present

people=happiness because
people = love

happiness is doing what you want
being who you are
without fear of judgment
ridicule, degradation, and disrespect

happiness is the freedom to
just be whatever it is
that pleases you to be

this does

Like a cactus
I think of you

moon cascades
your auburn hair to shoulders

a peyote button
brooch for adventurers

rising up
parted lips in ecstasy

desert thirsts for rain
longing for you

Traveling on light
an atom
a quark
a seeker journeying into
transcendental worlds

Jim traveled light
free
unencumbered
chance encounters the goal

seek (that's twice) and find
share
propagate
expand the awareness of
fellow journeymen

Slip slide
into a puddle seven miles wide
flirt squirt
your seed upon her skirt

take the ferry to the other side
a bamboo chalet you shall reside
come, you must abide
tune in, turn on, enjoy the ride

Xanadu, for you, dining on honeydew
like Liefson, Lee, and Peart, to name a few
forty-two, a Douglas wrote for you
hitchhike, a query asked, nothing for you to do

but not the end
my mind is all dried
the synapse fried
I tried

I witness my life as if a dream
unfolding before my eyes
imagination unfurling in minutes,
hours, days, weeks, years
the only reality is the
programs I behold on my television
it is there I truly reside
those characters my real friends
to view is to live
and upon their ending
so is mine

What does it mean to be happy?
I have forgotten
why is it so difficult for me?
how does one go about it?

oh, woe is you
poor sad sack
listen for the violins
snap out of it

I would if I were able
it is exhausting feeling as I do
I bore even myself
with these dramatics

as you should
you sniveling fool
stop your whining and focus on what is good
you should feel so blessed

and yet
no matter how I try
I don't

Behind the glass
the flickering fantasy
becomes my reality

it is here I wish to linger
to remain
until the arrival of my friend

why does he take so long?
what purpose is the delay?
I wait and gaze

I am smitten, infatuated
but for why?
it's pointless, its pulse moves in one direction

I wait
caught between this and that
one I have, one I long for

and my friend still tarries
his sight beckons
but does not claim

though I long for the embrace of eternity
nothing hastens his arrival
his grim face avoids me

I sit
legs dangling above six feet of empty earth
viewing what I wish for even more

ACKNOWLEDGED

You look up
our eyes meet
you nod
you acknowledge me
I exist
you see me
but also not
still I pass through
automatic doors don't open
was I here?
but you did see me
I saw you more

This is shit
let the critics receive their validation
but it must be extracted
often ladled from the surface
but purged none-the-less
if only to soothe my own sense of self-worth
ironic, I realize
they are my emotions
        my thoughts
        my fears
        my feelings
they are yours now
to do with as you please
my role is to share
yours may be to compost

Can you see me?
can you hear me?
do you acknowledge I exist?

I am here!
I am calling you!
I am trying to connect with you!

we could be happy
we could find love
together we could be united

The darkness descends like an old friend
the cool embrace inviting
"walk with us," it says
"stay with us," it beckons

shrouded, eyes wide yet unseeing
shortsighted/blinded
lost but at peace
familiar
dare it be said?
comforting

occasional rays of light
glimmers of hope
has the day finally arrived?
if so, only to linger a few hours

To shimmer so
a beauty's glow
radiant light
a heart set alight

my pulse quickens
my tongue thickens
eyes bedazzled
a nerve left frazzled

oh, to have your gaze
a thought to amaze
your love a desire
a hope none higher

my quest to feel love so
a dream, I know
one I hope not to wake from
a reality to soon come?

A million miles away
yet feet apart
only one aware of the other
only one filled with desire
me for you

a million miles away
standing next to me
different perceptions
different universes
me, lost in a black hole
separated
alone
adrift

beep, beep, beep
I've completed scanning my items
Thank you for the assistance

It's magical
though I see her
it's like she doesn't exist
a pepper's ghost

her beauty
nothing so cliché
as to say it radiates
more so, emanates

is she an illusion?
there but unreal
like a mirage
a fantasy, again cliché

oh, but to write of beauty such
oh, but to realize the dream of love
oh, but to write a poem of love

She looks upon me
with her dewy eyes
with the same passion and interest
as one would
a Styrofoam plate at a picnic
worthy of loading with potato salad
a utility
and soon to be claimed
by the rubbish bin
worth spent

the idea of a romantic encounter
as foreign to her
as a farm chicken
running in the Olympics
in a 500-meter sprint

I make myself sick
trying to be healthy
the poison
is the medicine

we say do not murder
but we do it anyway
we say do not behave like that
it's abnormal
but we do it anyway
we say that's illegal
but we do it every day
so, it all becomes normal
we try to convince ourselves it's not

we're wrong

I am miserable
in my happiness
I am discontented
in my contentment
I am depressed
in my mental health

two sides
same person
yin
yang
opposing
supporting

oh, to be united
with self
to find peace
amidst the struggle
one day
maybe

When you don't give a shit
that's when others notice
and begin to give a shit
but you can't notice
because you can't give a shit
so, others get mad
that you don't give a shit
that now they do give a shit
because you don't give a shit

get it?
If not
I don't give a shit

THE ABUNDANCE OF BLESSING

There is so much to do
so many stories to tell
marks to make
songs to sing
designs to design
books to read
music to hear
sights to see
but there is not enough time
all art is infinite
we will never be able to create it all
there's no way to produce the infinite
the very unmeasurable amount of art
is outpaced by the eternity of time
this abundance of blessing crushes me
its infinite weight presses to never-ending depths
dooms me to desperation and unquenchable depression
at my inability to capture the infinite

Focus only on the art
then mastery arrives
the act of creation
the sole purpose for the act
but this myopic vision
stirs the attention of fame
clouding the singular sight
a shift in focus
the voice is lost
vision diminished
hope survives only in the desire to regain mastery
obtained only when pursued individually
drawing adulation, vultures to carrion
tempting the artist as sirens
to drown the voice
if the heart gets lost
fame cannot be the desire
for art demands monogamy

JUST ONE

Just one hour to do this
then one hour to do that
just one more hour
maybe 24
just 48
but the need for hours never ends
there's always need for just one more
the clock keeps ticking
time will run out
and I will still need
just one more hour

THE QUESTION

To consume
or to create
that is the question
whether it is nobler
to be well-read
or well regarded

and in the inquiry
the answer
comes forth
and you have
consumed it

If the world won't behave as I want it
I shall build a world where it will

then the first world will recognize the beauty
of the second
and so, desire to become as second is

world building
can change the world it is built in
like the rings of Atlantis
the first circles the second
only to be so then encircled by the second

There is so much in this world to see
too much for two eyes
infinite lifetimes would still miss
the infinite
nothing is static
but one can see
what stands before one
capturing one infinite moment
making finite
yet even in the finite
one only need look closer, deeper
to discover
the molecular
infinity
once again

I'm a tourist
mental wandered
astral projector
transient
soon gone
a wisp
in infinity
as wind
passing
invisible
traceless
as if
never here

I am nobody
my words make no sound
like a tree falling in the woods
I am nobody
invisible
moon shadows mask my existence
faint like morn dew by afternoon
and so, I
am nobody

The illness made him feel
like a balloon stretch to the point of bursting
the treatment made him feel worse
it truly was a case of picking your poison
what remedy does one have when
the two options both lead to pain and suffering
what recourse would you chose
when the only options are
the degree of discomfort

oh, modern medicine
have we truly advanced much from leeches
and potions?

Life is a contradiction
we are born only so we can die
we must experience pain
only so we can feel joy
sadness, to experience happiness
there is no meaning to anything
and that, in turn, becomes its meaning
life is a circle
a cycle
a non-sensical ring of contradiction and agreement
meaningless and pointless

having nothing to say, is saying
something
we do what they say can't be done
we accomplish what we're told we can't do

a world of contradictions
double standards, hypocrisy
scream for your rights
but don't allow others theirs

what are these things I write?
do my words move you?
should a poem ask more questions than it answers?
should it be self-referential?

the day ends in darkness
but the mind is alight with thoughts

MISSED CONNECTIONS

Did we just share a look?
it's so difficult for me to know

I'm desperate to make a connection
oh, that dreaded word desperate
you see it as a badge of dishonor
instead of empathizing with the need

left unchecked
it becomes all-consuming
because it is all one has

Fit a lifetime into one day
don't let one second get away
every second counts
not a moment to spare
the tension mounts
will you produce your share
dream it
create it
post it
make your mark
don't miss your chance
don't let the moment pass
even this moment counts
make it worth it

is it?

It's a fine line
between being a sensitive artist
and a whiny pratt

it's hard not to feel
like the whole world is against you
when you play by the rules
yet still get ignored

what do you have to do
to get a little respect round here?
is that too much to ask?

or am I just whining?

addendum:
if so,
fuck you!

THE DAY HAPPINESS DIED

Happiness stopped visiting when I was fifteen
there wasn't a specific event
we didn't have an argument
it was simply a gradual decline
in the time spent together
we became two ships passing in the night
we were aware the other was there
apparent that neither of us much cared
I miss happiness now
and her friend joy
they are often inseparable
so, when one left
the other followed
now I spend my time with new friends
I know they'll never leave me
or I, them
we pass our days quietly
contemplating life, the universe, and everything
it's just the three of us
loneliness, despair, and me

Life is messy
we strive so hard
like salmon against the current
thinking we can make it just right
only to discover that right is messy
it never ceases being fucked up
there are glimmers of joy
but it always returns to chaos
once we learn to embrace the mess
only then
can we sustain a prolonged
sense of freedom
the more you love the mess
the less mess there is

CONTRADICTIONS

The more I learn
I realize
the less I know
I fear
I shall learn my way
into oblivion

the more I work
the less I get accomplished
I shall work my way
into non-existence

I am so tired
yet have so much yet to get done
I am energized by accomplishment
but should I rest and recharge
or press on and burn out?

Though he desired to wring
every last drop from the day
darkness beckoned
a sweet call to unconsciousness
but it was the dawn
he longed to postpone
how ironic then
to struggle to keep eyes wide
to forestall the very thing
he desired most
deep oblivion
because its arrival hastened
his most feared event
waking

Every day is a battle
how cliché
yet cliches are forged
from truth
a struggle that will
never end
as infinite and eternal
as life itself
life is a battle
the battle is life
struggle to eat
struggle to make a living
struggle to find love
struggle to find peace
struggle to find joy
each day turning like soil
before a work
a life of compost
dying
yet
birthing new life
a ring
never-ending
cliché
yet true

Is this the scribbling of a raving lunatic?
but who would know?
scratching on a prison wall
of his own making
locked away
no eyes shall behold
loneliness the only audience
silence the only applause
the paper the only eyes
the ink the only voice
it cries out
hear me
see me
acknowledge me
as a flower to sunlight
the scribblings shout
I exist
I am here
I am not mad

There are moments of great fertility
the mind a bountiful garden
blooming thoughts
ripe with meaning
words as nectar
sweet to all ears
life-affirming
a soil teeming with nutrients
of song
        verse
                theme
                        prose
drink deeply of me
harvest the richness of words
seeded in seasons past
to produce such lush yield
it's for all to partake
to feast
        indulge
                satisfy
                        satiate

My language is accomplishment
no matter how small
the act of completion is the high
completion is victory
completion is overcoming
completion is satisfaction
every completion
washing the dishes
reading the paper
a job well done
a report turned in
a project approved
a to-do list written
a contract signed
an email sent
a shopping list fulfilled
the mail read
a sale closed
a purchase made
a checklist checked
all is joy
even this simple poem
which is now complete

Contrary to some beliefs
the world is not ending
it's eternal
even when dead and dusty
it exists

the universe shall always be
like a tree falling unseen in the woods
if expanding
what is it expanding into?
something can't expand into nothing
and if the universe should end
what will come after?
even a void is still a void
the lack of something is still something

and as this poem concludes
it is still something
that once did not exist
but has now ended

THE ME TOO MONSTER

I can write that way,
me too
but you don't

I can paint that way,
me too
but you won't

I can sing that way,
me too
so why don't you?

I can act as good,
me too
where do you?

me too
me too
look at me and give me a chance
stand up and do it
stop talking about it and do it

like this?

IT'S ONLY

It's only TV
but it's our culture
and a mirror to our culture
like Schrodinger's cat
it is in both states at once

it's only music
but it gets us through tough times
and reflects our tough times
it's everything and nothing

you're only a social media influencer
but you do have influence
self-created from nothing
yet controlling minds

these are only words
but there's context
and subtext
they're basic and profound

it's only life
you live it once, you're done
a moment in eternity
yet so important in the moment

THE IF I ONLY MONSTER

The if I only monster sat in its cave all day
pondering and ruminating on why
things were the way they were
he was paralyzed by his pontification of how
things were
yet never, ever, ever attempted to change
things to how he preferred
it was much easier for the if I only to sit and complain
"if I only had all the time in the world,
oh, the things I could create."
"if I only could do it over again,
things would be different."
"If I only could talk to her, then she would realize…"
"If I only could do what I want,
then my genius would be recognized."
day in and day out he rationalized and
did bemoan his existence
without ever once stopping to think
the blame was his alone
and so, he lived the remainder of his days
alone in his cave surrounded by excuses
which only got in his way
if only he could see

the shorts

If you create art
and no one knows
or cares
is it still art?

Rounded peak
topped with fuzz
soft protuberances
projecting left and right
bulbous bulge
topographical landmarks
orifice trifecta
top of the heap
crowning glory
my head

I have something to say
regardless of if you want to hear it
regardless of if you agree or disagree
regardless of if you value it
I have something to say

there, I said it.

You're happy
then you're sad
you never stay
one thing forever

The act of creation
is the reason
closer to the one
was that His intention?

A wisp
fleeting
then gone
not gone
moving on
silent
undetected
but for a moment
then past
not remembered
or desired
my life

Magnum opus?
ha ha ha ha ha ha ha ha ha
ha ha ha ha ha ha ha ha ha
ha ha ha ha ha ha ha ha ha
ha ha ha ha ha ha ha ha ha
ha ha ha ha ha ha ha ha ha
ha ha ha ha ha ha ha ha ha
ha ha ha ha ha ha ha ha ha
ha ha ha ha ha ha ha ha ha
ha ha ha ha ha ha ha ha ha
ha ha ha ha ha ha ha ha ha
ha ha ha ha ha ha ha ha ha
ha ha ha ha ha ha ha ha ha
ha ha ha ha ha ha ha ha ha
ha ha ha ha ha ha ha ha ha
ha ha ha ha ha ha ha ha ha

you can't even write a poem

Who the fuck is that
looking back at me from the mirror?

I have hair
I'm not that old
my eyes haven't dimmed from decades of despair
who are you?
leave this place!
you're not wanted here
by anyone

Are we not but juicy morsels
divinely designed
to wither and spoil
as we toil away
our insignificant eternally spanning lives
floating in the infinite expanse of space
on a big blue marble

Just existing
is life
but not
a life
worth existing for

The woman I'm looking for
is not looking for me

Confusion
constantly
life
repetition
no reprieve
ambiguity
manic
confusion
association
poem

Sometimes tough love
is the only love to give

Beep
bip
doink
zip
flop
sploosh

these sounds I make to you
as a show of my love

for making stupid noises

what did you think I meant?

Sun dappled dust particles
drift lazily in swirls
lighting upon your skin
moist from action
morning exertion

The furrows are ripe with harvest
growing with ideas, concepts, stories, and images
growing non-stop
pollinating one another, each other
in a never-ending orgy of productive energy
the brain bursts forth
with a cornucopia of creativity

So much to do
so much to see
so much to say
so much to write
so much to read
so much to watch
so much to make
so many places to go
so many people to meet
so many things to try
so little time

See the man
see the lonely man
see the depressed man
see the man without hope
he is a hopeless romantic

All I want to do
is make love to you
all you want to do
is run away from me

How does one go on
lacking all desire too?
who is more selfish,
the person who wants to die,
or the person holding them back?

Puff puff
quiet now
reflection time
        upon
self dies
peace rises
awareness expands
so cliché, this
trite really
it doesn't help you write any better

Mental stability
balanced like golden rock pagoda
a wind blows
teetering dangerously
desperately clinging
to sanity

Life is not one size fits all
you'll have it your way
I'll have it mine
What's good for the goose
Is not always good for the gander

People are murdered
get rid of guns
people post hate and lies
get rid of social media
people pollute the air, water, and land
get rid of fossil fuels
maybe it would just be easier
to get rid of people

A breeze
shuddering shoulders
a faint sensation
am I
to you
then gone
at least glass
reflects
yet I
leave no remembrance

Life is what happens
while you're waiting
for life to begin

I ask too many questions
I know
but how else
do I show I care?

You fancy yourself a poet?
I acknowledge I am a creator of things
you think yourself a philosopher?
I perceive myself to have thoughts
you consider yourself enlightened?
I can only compare myself to you

I write lists of the
things I'm going to do
better than I do doing the
things I'm going to do

You worry about you
I'll worry about me
you'll worry about me
I'll worry about you
we can both worry
about the world

a bird in the sky
has no worries
as it passes by

Everything is artistic
        choice
live your authentic
        self
just be

there is no one
        way
there is only
        you
just be

let everything
        just be
let everyone
        just be
just be

Repeat repeat
don't make me say it twice
here we go again
deja vu
over and over
round and round
looping like a Celtic knot
continuous patterns
a rerun
echoing echoes

I'm doing the best I can

we demand more
we will not be satisfied

even this poem
does not quench the hunger

the longs

171

Muse, muse, a dead muse
it's all a ruse

Jim rides a Cadillac into a
bloody Mary sunset

and vine, the crossroads
oh, the humanity

chesterfield is calling
such a regal name

Lewis, did you call Carroll?
if not, you'll lose your head

lose your head
lyrics of the queen

couplets singing
riding moonbeams to moon pies

no sense in making nonsense
it's all just for play

follow the white rabbit
follow the thoughts in your head

no need to rewrite
if it seems right in your head
there's still a rhythm

in its randomness

can you feel it? can you feel it?
its pulse tapping morse code on the inside of your skull

a fever flamingo dance
between crows on the wing

the lady can sure sing
a rabbit trail of white

you bring sense to this web
it's yours now. the end

27 letters
in which
to create with

27 letters
thousands of
combinations

and this is what
I came up with

syllable
nouns and verbs
adjectives and adverbs

27 letters
constellations
galaxies and solar systems

27 letters
formations
like geese migrating

quatrains
stanzas and meter
blank verse

only 27 letters
to share
all my feelings

how can the infinite
and eternal
be depicted in 27 letters?

My problem
among others
is I believe
life is a problem
to be solved
not lived
at least
not until
the problem
has been
solved
and that
in turn
produces
a problem

here's another
is this
a poem
or just a sentence
broken up
dramatically?

everything
becomes
a conundrum
for me
which is
one of life's
problems

and that is
a problem
for me
worth solving

I circle round
in logical spirals
or spirals of
illogic
thinking
I'm so clever
ever so
meta
but maybe
it truly is clever

and yet again
I'm faced
with solving
the problem
of life
that's my problem

We're taught to conform
then we celebrate the non-conformists
the more they non-conform
the more we honor them
so, it becomes their non-conformity
that conforms them to the honor

the less they care
the more we care
what they have to say
what they think
what they do
what they wear
who they date
what they eat
so, the trend becomes
not to care
but then you care about making sure
you look like you don't care

even raging against the machine is played out
it's jumped the shark
when a band makes raging against the machine
their name
raging against the machine has simply become
the machine
the band's popularity reinforces the theorem

but we still have too then
rage against the new machine

of rage which should be an outrage
but it only becomes all the rage

lift them up
so we can tear them down
praise them
so we can destroy them

Icarus of celebrity

award them
so we can cancel them
honor them
so we can disavow them

a cruel game
we make celebrity
only to chastise them
for all we wanted from them in the first place

what a cruel joke
what a wicked prank
what an evil society

we make our heroes
so we can tear them down
build them
tear them down
just to build them up
so we can tear them down again

we are cruel
to be kind
we bless
only to curse
for being so blessed
which becomes a curse to them
but they claim to be so blessed

how can joy and success
only bring pain and hardship?
win the lotto
only to become bankrupt
achieve your dream
only for it to become your nightmare
when success becomes your prison
our athletes succeed once
so, they must succeed every time
it's all to nothing
gold or go home
if you're not winning
you're losing

but success breeds success
wealth attracts wealth
when you have money
you no longer need it
things are given to you for free
yet the poor starve
success only to attract destruction
through overindulgence

the success precipitates
the destruction
like flies on a carcass
then we celebrate it
with documentaries and tributes

we get clean
only to get dirty
we relapse so we can overcome
a cautionary tale
which becomes the normality

we seek fame and notoriety
only to act like it's no big thing
we act like we're too cool for fame
then that becomes what we are famous for

I've just got to be me
but if me doesn't conform
then me is rejected and scorned
but if me is an artist
then non-conformity is me
but if I'm not perceived as an artist
then non-conformity is seen
as immature and unprofessional

we celebrate nonconformity in
Ricky Powel, David lynch, Jim Morrison, and more
but ridicule it in others

sour grapes or truth?
envy or honesty?
there is no one measurement
there is no one rule

come up from nothing
pull yourself up from your bootstraps
then reinforce your position with a posey
the gatekeepers
the entourage
but you're just one of the boys
you're from the hood
you're human, just one of us

but you're too good for the hood
you've made your way out
moved on up
don't look down
don't look back
except to claim your street cred
you pose, you flex
that's your new cred
guard it with your life
behind your gates and security
nothing like the hood

why shouldn't you enjoy your fame
indulge in the benefits of your success
you worked hard to get where you are
then don't claim you aren't who you've become
you've gotten soft
the streets washed off
you can act like a G
but an OG is no longer a G
you can front
respect will let it go
truth is, youth just indulging
while at the same time honoring
often with lip service
portrayed as heartfelt

cynical or serious
jealous or investigating
sad truth
I want to be one of them
but not one of them
which only makes me one of them
but not one of them
class system
caste system
doesn't seem to have much class to them
hierarchy
social construct
by a society
we want to be a part of

The dead
haunt us
whether they know it
or not

their spirit
transcends
and lingers in the form
of our memories

no matter
your belief
there is a spirit
in some form

the dead
can transfigure
from any time period in history
taking any past form

that is spirit
eternal form
of a mortal body
like Schrodinger's cat

I miss
my dad already
every memory of you
from life and deterioration

I write
these words
to honor you while also
to heal

you're welcome
to haunt me
I cherish each memory
of a moment with you

your spirit
transcended
but your spirit is still
here with me
Hide in my shell
hide in my asylum
become lost in minutia

build the wall
build the cocoon
protection from you all

erect the barrier
erect the fencing
keep the world at bay

I'm safe here now
I'm safe from hurt
I'm alone but safe

Searching
A quest for significance
Uncensored
Unedited

Sophomoric
Profound
Meta
Self-referential

Planned & purposeful
A style created
Found
Like cast iron

Questioning
While birthing
A fabrication
One letter at a time

Where is the curator?
Whom can we blame?
Is there no editor?
The answer stares back at you

First draft
Second draft
A thousand drafts
What does it matter?

We celebrate demos
As much as remixes
Which is the true art
Art is the creation

This has gone on long enough
This exploration
Exhortation
A decision must be made

It ends
When just knowing
As in
Now
Is it really so hard?
you'll live through it
why is it so difficult for you?
you'll come out on the other side

life is full of ups and downs
season and cycles
ebbs and flows
that's why we have so many idioms (and poems)

you'll live
if it doesn't kill you, it'll make you stronger
if you're walking through the valley
        of the shadow of death
don't stop

so why be so dramatic?
you've made it this far
you've learned and grown
you're a better person because of it

so, carry on
what else you got to do?

THE LONG AND RAMBLING ROAD

Black custard pie
coursing veins ruminate
pulsate, ejaculate, propagate

toasted artichoke heart
infected organ's remorse

escaping into madness
will you follow?
rhythm lost

metastasized mushroom
where are you going with this?
meta self-referential
lazy but often imitated

this took a turn
ears ringing
not church bells
off rails
yet still driving
pistons pumping
go, boy, go!
we're with you – you have our support

cry out, cry
let ink be your soul
freeform
midnight norm
stream of ink

write don't think
suddenly new meter

style curved like a diseased spine
another curve
time elapse
during thought escape
it's all just drivel
honestly?
you think this will matter?
you are mad as a hatter

your marks
are unremarkable
clever to you
but who are you to say?
so biased
so desperate
you suckle on the teat
of validation

Venus has shunned you
not even turning her back
simply looking through you
a plate of glass
no emotion streaks your surface
greasy swill runs in street gutters
back to nonsense
not poetry
desperate symbolism

to obscure to be cared for
messy metaphors
poor prepositions
amateur! critics cry
no retrospective collection in your future
egotist
to even think it
then to write it
but no one will know
for no one will care
to even seek that it exists
that you even exist
you poor self-absorbed
black custard pie

CONTRADICTION

Nothing is what it says it is
you can't generalize
contradiction
truth
rail against fascism
then limit free speech
set up registries
all in the fight against fascism
to win
you must be fascist
believe in almighty god
then blow up a plane
a building
a courthouse
in his name
if you believe he's all-powerful
why does he need your help
contradiction
we want peace
we build weapons
to ensure it
contradiction
we seek love
unconditionally
then we set conditions
look this way
behave this way
support me this way
do this for me
or i withhold my love

we act in a way to offend
then get offended
that you're offended
contradiction
we yell and scream
to counter your yells and screams
we fight because
you started the fight
we bully
because we claim we are bullied
contradiction
we demand our rights
by taking yours away
you scream intolerance
and are intolerant of others
who don't believe as you
one source is propaganda
one is news
one claims truth
one screams, lies
both claim they're right
and they are
both are propaganda
both are lies
both shout, our side is right
and both sides are wrong
it never ends
it never changes
like a contradiction
it circles

and redirects
or does it?
maybe it is over
change is happening
yet it's not
it's all contradiction

The intentional
lack of meaning
is the entire meaning

the formless
mark for mark sake
is the form

it's purposelessness
devoid of symbolism
is its purpose

the lack of story
backstory or narrative
is the story

the unsophistication
rudimentary and crude
is the sophistication

breaking the rules
not adhered to by many
is the new rule

breaking the rules
is the rule
so, no rules

know the rules
to break the rules
some say

does it make it more impressive that way?

if you break a rule perfectly
without knowing the rule
does that make it imperfect?

who makes the rule?
did they know
rules are meant to be broken?

allow the words
to be heard
accept all who enter

crush the double standard
and prejudices
the class and caste system

let art be
for art's sake

Ambiguity

is there any truth anymore?
your truth
my truth
regression therapy
false narratives
propaganda
motives
who do you believe?
what do you believe?
how can you believe one thing?
and not another?
three sides to every story
yours, mine, the cold hard truth
doing your own research
makes you smarter
then those whose research
you read
everything is everything
and nothing at all
it is what it is
what does that even mean?
idioms
slogans
where's the truth?
whose truth?
Gregorian knots
twisted, ceaseless
cycling
gaslighting

censored
speaking your truth
the woke so woke
they become controlling and judgmental
the very thing they despise
when liberals ban books
the end is nigh
black and white
shades of gray
two-sides of the same coin
stereotypes reinforced
but still stereotypes
truth in lies
lies in truth
no one is unbiased
no objectivity
clear as mud
ambiguity
this is

Late night
early morning
create
pontificate
mentally masturbate

your words
written
paper deteriorates
the long dark night
who do you think you are?

these scribbles
brushes soiled
American dream
crucified
an ego died

nevermore justified
run and hide
die, die, pride
enough
rhyme and meter

feed the meter
your time
for all time
it comes in time
ahead of his time

enough!
narcissist
so clever
your meta
what will they think?

time tells all tales
hidden message
rhythm over substance
exposed as naught
a hard lesson taught

you're fraught
with self-loathing
while contradictory ego-maniacal
no rhythm there
you're a sham
but there's no one to care

Heavenward
sonic rhythm
time elapses
spiral conflations
gibberish and nonsense
no meaning
disguised as wise
pointless & futile
drivel of self-importance
and portend
porridge
the rhythm returns
no vortex of shame
only the pulse
of pronouns, nouns
syllables
without melody
yet music
lyrical
but not by rote
freeform
follow the rhythm
feel it now
pulsating
endless
infinite
ongoing
now just boring
I'm snoring
but you're just being crass

lowbrow
not for the literati
new rhythm
it is ongoing
do you feel it?
thump, bump, thump
rhyme, literation, metronome
freestyle
improvisation
eternal
syllables = beats
bpm
boundless pulse momentum
it's words
it's rhythm
feel it?
feel it.
follow along
or start your own
add to the music of the universe
too cliché?
lens pointed at lens
fisheye
don't distract
the root is exposed
get to the heart of the matter
don't use idioms
a new rhythm
inappropriate
we've been here before

redundant?
homage
series & style
so meta
so your thing
here he goes again
will it ever end?
no
go back to the start
follow along
or start your own
impossible
the wave has already departed the station
the infinite is always infinite
infinitely
overreach
or mastery?
insecure
or dominating?
infinite questions
infinite jest
can't ride on coattails with a reference
takes more than that
to be immortal
infinite
part of the flow
the rhythm
which has found its end
infinitely

MONDAY, FEBRUARY 22, 2021

One
I'm the problem
I may be correct
But wrong
Not allowed feeling
For fear of hurting another's
Don't speak out
To listen to others speaking
Die to self
So others can be themselves
I'm the problem

Two
Too many opinions
Too many, right
Others wrong
No correct
Just left and right
Us   them
Me   you
For centuries
We know
But never change
No one willing
Even though
We all lose

Three
Maybe it's better not to feel
Feelings just cause stress
Lead to strife
If numb
No one gets offended
No one gets hurt
Not me
I do not feel

But this proves I do
Can't write this if I don't
And the interpretation
Will cause pain
Best not to write it at all
Certainly, don't show it to anyone
Maybe it is best not to feel

Four
Be happy
Be happy
Do it
Do it now
Be happy
Be happy
Stop depression
Just stop
Be happy
Be happy
It's a choice

Make it
Be happy
Be happy
I'm sorry
I tried

Five
Save me
From myself
Or, more poetic
From self
To be saved
reverse rhythm more of class
saved I must be
from self
oh, high literature
of thy self
save away from me
the literati so cheer
but I perish
never saved

Six
of self-righteous
so downtrodden
wake, wake
from your own pity
and flagellation
oh, poor miser
so weary are thee

arise, arise
you self-loathing wretch
of self I speak

Seven
to thine own self be true
unless thine own self is me

Eight
don't speak of your own demons
don't write of your demons
ignore them
hide them
deny them
for others to discover
for others to decipher
you self-improvement hack
you self-referential twit
no one cares
oh pity me
no one bothers
cry for self
no one reads
so then stop
but one can't
the demons drive on
a hard boss to serve
a hidden force of power

The tormented artist lives on

Nine
I look through teenage eyes
Weathered with age
Seen as other, elder
Not human nor equal
Respected/
Not considered
Tolerated
Yet, I look through teenage eyes

All of life is a contradiction
a lie
we say things
make arbitrary rules
then break those very rules
and call it art
you can't mix antiques with contemporary
it's forbidden
yet
it is done
and becomes earth-shattering, cutting-edge design

you can't use certain bourgeoisie fabrics
the horror
but if you spray it metallic
using it ironically
suddenly – viola—
it is transformed into the chic
if it is that simple
wasn't it tre chic all along?

who determines it was one thing
or another?
when does primitive, childish, and pedestrian
suddenly become high-art?
if it is for one person
then, logic says
it is for all
unless some are better than others
decided on by some arbitrary judging panel

appointed by themselves
thus rendering the entire existence
as illogical, pointless, and meaningless
then if the illogical becomes the standard
then doesn't that illogic become logic?
and then, by that logic
anyone creating anything, breaking any rule
is thus creating art and something worth the collective
attention

society vs the citizens
society established to make some feel
more important than the rest
for what reason?
vanity?
the shame of such act should be greater
than the reward

THE MANIFESTO

Everything is art
bluechip
pop
low
broad
contemporary
design
toys are art
furniture is art
the clothing you wear
the food you eat
we celebrate singers
        their voice is their art
we celebrate architects
        their space is their art
we honor graphic design
        your menu
        you GUI
we honor entertainment
        your movies
        your books
we cover our walls in wallpaper
we cover our floor with rugs
we eat it
        drink it
        wear it
        hear it
        see it
        create it
art is everywhere

it's everything
the shoes you wear
the hair on your head
the skin on your body
we crave it
we pay for it
we collect it
we treasure it
we write about it
we read about it
it is itself
it is like carbon –
        a foundational element of life
the games we play
the words we say
everything is art

even this

We all just want to feel
like we mean something
like we have value
worth
we make a difference
our life has meaning
purpose

nothing new,
right?

but why then does it persist
this feeling we don't
I don't
no matter what i do
no one notices
no one cares

we all want to feel important
yet we all keep others from
feeling that way
or we resent them if they do succeed
we hold power over others
withholding our likes and hearts

and why does it matter anyway?
shouldn't we do something
just for ourselves
because we love it
our worth doesn't come

from other's approval
it comes from within

yet we still need others approval
we secretly crave it
like a drug habit
it infects our happiness
corroding our hearts
we know it
yet we do it
we hate it
and ourselves for desiring it

we are as hypocritical
as those that withhold from others

we are a race of hypocrites
selfish, conceited, unresponsible
a trifecta of sadness

Do
strive for more
push yourself
reach for the success
it's the way we do it
how the system works
how you play the game
grab the brass ring
aim for the moon
shoot for the stars
be the best
be number one
pr
good press
headlines
top ten lists
no rest for the weary
give it one hundred and fifty percent
winners don't quit
try and try and try again
pick yourself up from the bootstraps
pick yourself up and dust yourself off
win at all costs

unless you just can't
you can't catch a break
you're not allowed up to bat
you're stuck sitting on the bench
always on the sidelines watching the play go by
always the bride's maid, never the bride

the doors are closed in your face
they're locked from the inside
you struggle just to make ends meet
the deck is stacked against you
your turn never comes
your number is never called

but

you "need" to overcome
you "need" to carry on

how?

To come full circle
from the beginning
to never-ending
end

start
learn from your mistakes
start again
do over
move on
circle back
move forward
learn from the past
eye on the future

there's no way off
the merry-go-round of life
round and round you go

go round for another spin
the wheel of life
my head is spinning
fractal nature

just gibberish
yet truth
black
and white
turn off
to be turned on

sense
found in nonsense
truth
found in fiction

there's no stopping
so, enjoy the ride

Ideas swim
like koi in a pond
piercing the surface
gaping mouths
gulping air and
searching for nourishment

concepts grow
like crystals
rich in sediment and minerals
fractal forms
endless permutations
manifesting in perpetuity

aspiring to be
historic before their birth
one day maybe
but not today
have to walk
before you're memorialized

there's a process
but it's all worthy
only in hindsight
at first, discarded
later celebrated
time provides perspective

the meter has changed
like a demo to a single
iterations finding soil
rehearsals for days
through exploration, it's found

this word
this sound
this image
this mark

Walking cliché
there's always some reason
for not getting it done

excuses, excuses

then even if
you did publish your work
no one would read it

unrequited, unrequited

was it poetic enough
maybe you'll be appreciated
when your dead

unappreciated, unappreciated

will these words
ever matter?
will anyone ever care you wrote them?

unconfident, unconfident

is this Introspection
poetic
or sophomoric, pathetic?

insecure, insecure

the cycle is unceasing
the words come
but along with them, doubt

Everything is connected to everything
whatever happen was meant to be
it is
what it is
and what it is
is what it should be

how can it be
anything other than
what it is
when what it is
is what it should be

we are who we are
because that's
who we are
who we always were
who we always should be

how can you be
anyone but you
if you are
who you are supposed to be

we make life
so difficult
but maybe a hard life
is the only
life there is

we are a fractal origami
forever folding in on ourselves
perpetually folding tighter
only to expand infinitely

we are
we always have been
we always will be

I write these words
will they one day
be heard?

no matter anyway
it's all just pointless
we all pass away

ashes to ashes
dust to dust
these words are and will be

they contain my feelings
contain my soul
but lack any meaning

man will come
man will go
we return from whence we came

the pandemic becomes
the endemic
a new normal forms

we return to a life
with death and disease
and the usual strife

we accept the new norm
it becomes comfortable
we learn to conform

and still, these words I write
emptying my heart
all for naught, so goodnight

I make a trek
every day but Sunday
six days a week
every week
it's a short journey
not even a hundred paces
to and from
I make the trek
in sunshine, rain, and snow
some days I journey forth
more than once
always anticipating
excited like a child
at Christmas time
and when I return
empty-handed
I'm crushed
do I exist?
does anyone know I'm here?
there are certain days
I don't venture forth
there's no need
I know there's nothing
waiting for me
these are sad days
once or twice
I may forget
and I go forth anyway
only to be faced
With emptiness

a void
I often enjoy
the journey
taking in the sun
the fragrance on the wind
other times
I'm rushed
just want to get there
and back
through it all
my mailbox is a
chamber of wonders

MY GIRL

There is a girl
head covered in curls
to say I love this girl
there's not enough love in the world

I love her more
then bees love honey

she sings like a bird
no sweeter sound to be heard
her laughter pure joy
like a child with a new toy

I love her more
then bankers love money

she'll break my heart one day
there is no other way
she's not meant to stay
a new man will take her away

I love her more
then apes love bananas

it's the cycle of life
for her to be a man's wife
as I walk her down the aisle
I'll paint on my smile

I love her more then
flowers love rain

I couldn't be more proud
no regrets to shroud
her joy is my goal
my breaking heart the toll

I love her more
then feet love socks

there goes that girl
with head covered in curls
she's found a new love, this girl
and I must release her into the world

All life is in dual states
we are all Schrodinger's cat

she's the perfect wife
if only she wasn't a nag
he's the perfect husband
if only he wasn't such a pig

it's the perfect job
if only it paid what you're worth
it's the perfect home
if only it didn't need so many repairs

perfect
yet broken
dual state
at once

we are happy
if only we had this one thing
we have everything we want
if only we had that too

we are binary
ones and zeros
on and off
simultaneously

we want to be happy
if only we weren't depressed
we want to be satisfied
if only we didn't want it all

we live in two states
awareness and deceit
like a skittle
sweet and sour

Consideration not considered
banshees yowling in the streets
fight for rights
but who is?

demonic leaders don't lead
fanning flames
rhetoric screeched from the parapets
offense intended

winds change
empathy dies like a feral dog in an alley
no one notices
fetid souls

compassion was stopped
by jackboots in the promenade
the jackals applauded
flesh draped from barred teeth

the future will be canceled
the culture determined
to sentence every person
cancel each other

vultures soar circles over humanity's corpse

cnn, fox, msnbc
putrefied regurgitation for the masses
cause then report

responsibility died in its sleep
hearts hardened by partisanship
but yea for our side
bathed in the blood of generations yet born

it's over
the milk has been spilled on the cold linoleum
        of society
baked by the sun
curdled and sour

THE PROCESS OF WRITING

Writing is simply problem-solving
every word a decision every sentence a choice
each piece in the puzzle
to select the correct
      word
      phrase
      turn of
each is a problem in search of a linguistic solution
or, each is a problem to be solved
by a linguistic solution
see?
which is the proper solution?
which choice should be made?

creativity is, in truth, thousands upon thousands
of individual solutions
culminating in one collective solution
the writer must toil and labor
weighing each choice
for each word has
      meaning
      power
      purpose
multiple of words offer a multitude of meaning
so, each must be
      considered
      weighed
      investigated
      with studious intention
~~so that the essence [correct understanding]~~

so that the writer's goal is portrayed
the problem of purpose, intent, and meaning
must be solved with each choice of
        word
        sentence
        structure
this has been ~~the~~ a solution
to the problem ~~to explain~~ of explaining
the process of writing

TOMB OF PULP

The pages stacked up
no one did care
the sheets with scribbles and words
sat in darkness with no fanfare

word upon word
drawing upon drawing
work upon work

all for one audience
an audience of one
solely for one soul
not for lack of want to be seen
to be heard
to be cherished
and adored

yet the world turned its back
closed tight the lids
blocked out any recognition or acknowledgment
no matter how he tried
no matter what he produced
no matter how prodigious the output
no matter
that was how it was received
as if it were no matter
yet how could this be?
the evidence is clear
an abundance of riches
of no perceived value

yet still, he produced
page upon page of which
this is one
a tomb he created
of pulp
ink
paint
verse
script

What is the one thing no one escapes,
and no one understands?
death
it comes for us all
some welcome it
some face it in fear
with every passing day
its arrival grows nearer

what do we have to fear
when death comes to us
to take our hand and guide us
on a new journey
of darkness or everlasting light
of oblivion or repetition
of dust or immortality
when it comes
there is no argument
no negotiation
no parley
it comes when it wants to
no matter if you're ready

death isn't a he or she
it knows not of love
compassion
tenderness
or care
it simply does what it does
when it does it

bringing one life to an end
without prejudice
without malice
simply does

simply is

midnight musings

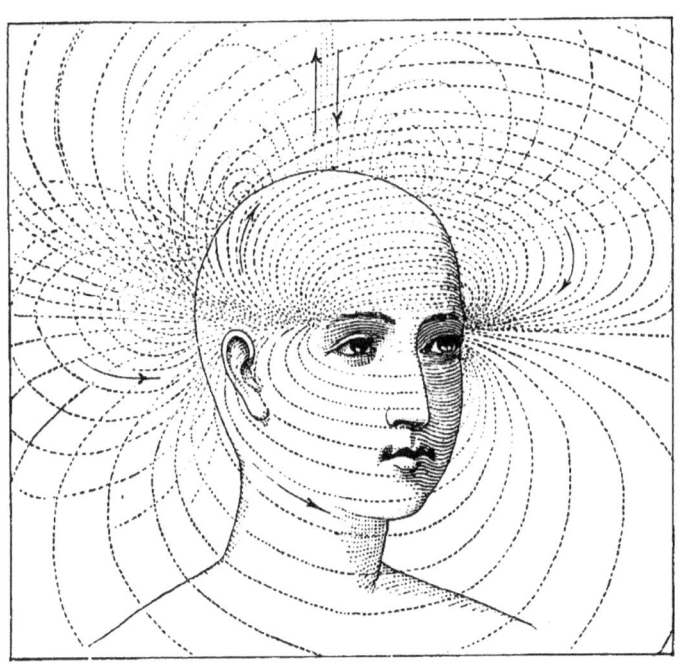

It's past midnight
New Year's Eve
2022
words stir like a dirty martini
as roman candles crackle
in the cool new year's sky

the pen crosses empty desert of pad
scarring page with ink
forms without meaning
without function
like stones blown across salt flats

the heater disrupts
the winter quiet
blowing hot air
like this author
why continue?
how do I stop?

rivers can be dammed
minds cannot

A mob rushing the stage
the mind amplified
break down the barricade

migration of neurons
pulsing, pulsating
an inherent drive
the soul knows what it knows

these words
the call of nature
midnight ramblings

drives one mad
drives one to create
to quiet the swarm
if only for a time

the time it took
to write this

Midnight rambler
evening toker
sweet evergreen
exposes the universe unseen

midnight wordsmith
mental mist
turn a phrase
leave mark on a page

midnight morning
stanza forming
release the valve
emotional salve

nothing is ever perfect
I write like an addict
words filling veins
some happy some pained

critics and fans
which will you be
when these words and rhymes
you read?

Late night rambler
Take a puff
Mental scrambler
That's the stuff

Eyes droop low
Like autumn leaves
You lost your rhyme
You lost your meter

Meaningless words pour out
First draft writer
A weak attempt to shout
Should all be christened with a lighter

Reflect what you desire
But I digress
My mind on fire
A midnight mental mess

Eyes reflect the
Written word
You found your rhyme
You found your meter

Midnight static
desire for greatness
desire for meaning
desire for substantiality
desire for recognition

egotistical mindset
this desire
false humility
to say they're just scribbles
maybe it's a demo

let it be
wasn't written in a day
it wasn't birthed
in perfection
it matures with repetition

how do you be
before being?
there's always a beginning
maybe, this is it

Words they flow
spinning tales
no one to show
the midnight writer

liquid words
blemish virgin pulp
regrets afterward
dissipate like vapor
the midnight writer

keep on pressing
breakthrough on the horizon
mind stressing
open mind lets the flies in
the midnight writer

driven by thought rot
madness knocks
it's all for naught
the critic balks
the midnight writer

set the pen down
rest your weary head
before the breakdown
don't worry you'll soon be dead
midnight writer

PROFOUND THOUGHTS AT MIDNIGHT

In 2021
the only response to
any statement is
who says?
followed closely by
why?

ad infinitum

there are no conclusions
only perceptions
there are no facts
only speculations
there are no truths
only opinions

who says?
why?

Midnight masquerader
fictional extraordinaire
alone
mental octane

keep on writing
keep on iterating
exemplary
in own mind

midnight muser
tablet ruminator
filler
review unworthy

keep on posting
keep on dreaming
noteworthy
in own mind

the masquerade
comes off at dawn

Midnight
the muse awakens
the question of why
haunts and protests
tormented mind, soul, heart
deep desires
unrequited

unquenchable
the mind driven mad
the heart dampened
pulse and flutter
broken spirit, trust, heart
infinite longing
unrequited

Midnight whispers
ruptured eardrums
with their taunts and criticisms
and can you blame them?
52, who are you?
why are you here
why do you make things so difficult?
like this

rest your head now
be comforted by night's blanket
you're alone
as always
but we're with you
taunt and criticism
always by your side
we comfort you while you sleep
put down the pen
close your eyes now
we'll meet again in the morning

Scribble, scrabble
dribble, babel
midnight ramble

girl, I think I'm so clever
love me for my brain
the rest of me
down the drain

too easy
that rhyme
this drivel
not worth the time

what a farse
this poem here
not even meta
can cause a reader to care

put the pen down
step away from the pad
a crime has been committed
ink has been spilled

Billy would be proud
you turned it on the crowd
a twist for an end
now, put down the pen

Do what you want to do
create the way you want to create

history is marked
with the celebrated remains of creatives
once obscure
now revered

do what you want
be free
you are limitless
boundaryless
to those that say you can't
look at all those that still did
that now you laud

www.ingramcontent.com/pod-product-compliance
Lightning Source LLC
LaVergne TN
LVHW051515070426
835507LV00023B/3132